First published by Botsotso in 2025
59 Natal St
Bellevue East
Johannesburg 2198
botsotsopublishing@gmail.com
www.botsotso.org.za

ISBNs:
Print: 978-1-7764952-0-7
e-book: 978-1-7764952-1-4

in the text©Abu Bakr Solomons
illustrations©Glen Arendse

Acknowledgements:

Many thanks to Glen Arendse for use of his drawings

Layout and design: Advance Graphics

And so, we begin to live again,
We, of the damaged bodies
And assaulted minds.
Starting from scratch with the rubble
of our lives.
And picking up the dust
of dreams once dreamt.

Starting over – fighting back
Sheila Cassidy

CONTENTS

	PAGE
Yielding	1
Goodbye	2
Syria	3
Saskatchewan, Canada	5
Voyage	6
Kraalbaai	8
Athlone sprees	9
It's almost enough	10
The guava stew that spurned death	13
This day, Sharpeville	14
Signposts during a time of isolation	15
Death of a journalist	16
Weekend in Langebaan	17
A pedagogy for defiance	18
The imam who died	20
Warrior	23
How memories are made	24
Pax Americana	25
Questions and answers behind walls	26
Remembering me	29

New South African phobias	30
Reforms, regress	31
Non-delivery stagnation	32
Passing time	33
Train rides with Sasja	34
Wall of denials	36
After the fall	37
Lumumba's tooth	39
What kind of life is this?	40
Schoolboy	41
Burying IAC	42
Jerusalem	43
No longer a quiet place	44
Hungry people dream	45
Sinecures and hustlers	47
Tomorrow's jailer	48
A day becomes, in so many ways	49
B.......... light	50
Paused to see the beauty	53
The rubble of our lives	54

YIELDING

Looking into the eyes of your children as they frolic
playing for your attention,
I witness how we have multiplied.

Your wives, rounded like mature tree trunks,
have yielded a few branches,
are rooted and steadfast.

GOODBYE

Sunday ends with piles of plates, leftovers –
mutton curry and *roeti* heaped in the sink;
what lies around, signs of goodbye.

You take your basket of laundry,
a suitcase with clothes from the boot of my car,
implying checking will occur somewhere else, *sans* us.

New interests entice you to leave the familiar;
you will reflect where nightfall lulls memories
and snow freezes yesterdays.

SYRIA

I am there with you, Syria,
wading through your streets
as the television screams the sacrilege
of your devastation; I watch in a room
in my sad, embattled country,
mourning betrayals with you.

You have been violated, broken into dead fragments;
your lilting lyrics once inspired poets,
and keen craftsmen carved devotedly
where glorious villages once flourished;
your squares and majestic temples with studded domes
glittering in golden sunsets, all demolished.

Your tomes, that for thousands of years
stirred the hearts of pious devotees and scholars,
enlightening during a zenith of learning,
now charred heaps of ash,
scattered between defiled and burnt corpses.
What did you desecrate to inherit the carnage
tainting your azure skies and soaring minarets?

Submerged in the quagmire of a dictatorial dynasty,
you contract cunning corporates –
plundering platoons of devious men,
scavengers from dying empires –
to bury and camouflage heaps of rubble.

SASKATCHEWAN, CANADA*

Blood and bodies foul the land of the flowing river,
executions disconcert during the impending fall.
It's a season of vexing questions but hollow answers.

From where does this rage spiral, unleashing an orgy of slaughter?
Did the pope's recent mission to seek absolution for old followers
open old wounds – or was it a miasma of drugs?

Truth lurks in the two dead brothers, the Sandersons: **
silent corpses stretched in a morgue housing the underbelly
of Canada's reservations, home to resurging episodes of violence
perpetrated against indigenes.

Is this macabre vortex an aftermath of colonialist settlers'
plundering of fertile lands?
Are these demons, taunting and tormenting, human flotsam
of imperialist adventures?
Will the ghosts of complicity concealed under the façade
of Canadian urbanity finally emerge?

An Anglican priest reminds his congregation
of how the spectre of stolen lands haunts the holy hour.
(Did peace pipe negotiations bring settlement
to Azania? Yagan's land? Aotearoa?) ***
Trendy Trudeau subdues disturbed citizens
with eloquent speeches dictated by neo-colonial cliques.
It is they who triggered this bloody spree.

*territory of the Cree nation **Damian and Myles Sanderson
***South Africa, Yagan, Australian aboriginal freedom fighter, New Zealand

VOYAGE

I

We embarked on a maiden sea cruise
in this gigantic ship that resembles
a sixteen-storey floating hotel.

Sailing towards the Portuguese Islands,
the ocean swayed gently as the vessel
sliced through unfathomable depths with precision.

Travelling to undiscovered territory,
motion seemed to dominate the mystery.

II

In the *Belle Epoque*, the onboard restaurant
where we shared a dinner table
with Gert and Ansie from Ladismith,

we chatted about our new adventure,
children and grandchildren. First, they had five,
but now, Ansie said, only four are left –

one grandchild crushed to death
when a bridge under construction at school
collapsed on him – and Gert became quiet.

We learnt about it on the news, we said,
and there they were, the grandparents, relating,
as if the horror had not subsided.

III

Later we veered towards more comfortable conversation –
about the efficacy of cooking curry with fresh spices,
remedies to combat diabetes.

We returned home not knowing if we would ever meet again,
but a few days after the trip Ansie telephoned.
We happily chatted about our serendipitous meeting.

KRAALBAAI

Here, on the robust West Coast between dunes,
lie myriads of life's fossil fragments.
Strolling on its pearly sands, we watch a calm lagoon
gently ebbing and flowing below a sapphire blue sky.

Busy mice furtively scramble for our crumbs,
bold, grey-beaked gulls squawk, ranting at us
for failing to resolve our disagreements.
We slip on slimy eels slithering under our feet;
this makes us laugh, grab each other for support.

Filial affection, fragile, furtively fortifying again,
dissipating many months of acrimony,
promises to revive and renew broken bonds,
banish bitter bouts of ire and enmity.

ATHLONE SPREES

When I buy in Athlone,
many with whom I've shared colourful days
hobble into shops
with a querulous grandchild or two in tow.

Years have mapped faces,
sore knees, lumbago stiffened the gait,
but those discernible gestures and voices
are the bulwark for forgetfulness.

This embodied memory would have been lost
if I had succumbed to the cheap shelters of refuge
under sunless skies offered to the disenfranchised
in Europe and North America.

Athlone sprees now weigh the burden of forbearance
in my errant country;
encounters with old friends
remind that time is circular not linear.

IT'S ALMOST ENOUGH

It's almost enough for me …

to find your worn socks lying forlornly
in your wardrobe, an old teddy bear
with a heart tied around its neck,
the words *kiss me* written in red,
staring at me when I open the door.

It's almost enough for me …

to gaze at all the diplomas on the wall
remembering how we beamed
when you walked in
from your school's annual award ceremonies.

It's almost enough for me …

to hear you say, *I am holding you in my duahs,*
and I reply, *Me, too;*
to hear you promising, *I will visit you soon,*
and I respond, feigning to be nonchalant,
See you then, insha'Allah.

It's almost enough for me …

to walk into your empty room and not see
you sleeping safely in your single bed,
but stumbling across things you have left behind,
closing the divide between us.

It's almost enough for me …

to finally know that a goodbye was inevitable,
making it easier for both of us to realise
that while you are growing up,
I am growing old.

THE GUAVA STEW THAT SPURNED DEATH

In the morning, the ground is covered
with ripe guavas dropped from the tree.
Ravenous birds flock, pecking its bounty,
leaving us bitter peels and some fruit to harvest.

Now to prepare syrupy guava stew with sugar,
water and spicy cinnamon sticks in a pot,
the aroma suffusing the kitchen.
Of course, guava stew has to be enjoyed
with creamy, hot, yellow custard.

At four in the afternoon, I take a bowl to Ma
who is ninety-six years old,
ill in a Frail Care Centre for the aged,
recuperating from acute bronchitis.

She is lying on her bed when I spoon the guava stew
into her mouth like she's a baby.
She slurps it up, smiling, and announces gently:
I don't think I'll die today.
Maybe during the week, but not today.

THIS DAY, SHARPEVILLE

It is not only your child lying broken
on the side of the railway lines
naked, starving.

It is our child, too.

It is not only your defiled mother
dragged out of her home in Gaza,
estranged in the only country she knows.

It is our mother, too.

It is not only your father,
scarecrow on the pavements in the suburbs,
begging to be chosen for work.

It is our father, too.

It is not only your torn sister,
battered and violated in a field
as the sun sweeps over Monwabisi.

It is our sister, too.

Wherever someone is in torment,
homeless or hungry,
their anguish annihilates peace.

Yours, mine and ours.

SIGNPOSTS DURING A TIME OF ISOLATION

Winter departed surreptitiously:
rain and wind hushed
as vagrant sunbeams crept into days.

We could frolic in the ocean's tepid tides
that hardened our bodies
during chilly spells.

Many left, with scant ceremony,
while we waited thankful for safety,
still counted among the living.

We face days virtually sinking,
fidgeting and fussing with shadows
before sleep seals our isolation.

It's like ambling along a long road
without signposts; not knowing
when to turn or even pause.

We meander, foraging for a few chores,
routines to salvage time
by providing anchoring purposes.

DEATH OF A JOURNALIST

Do they believe they've muted you by razing your notebooks,
shooting a bullet through your head?
                                        Murder renders them blind.

The more an enemy distorts, the sooner a voice grows wings,
soars above machinations of unbridled cruelty.
Truth and courage triumph over plundering tanks, shoot down snipers,
                                      bewilder Western bullies.

Bulldozing villages into rubble, wanton erasure of the dispossessed
bears bitter fruit for children who will harvest chaos;
those resisting to sever chains are not the ones who are defeated,
                                    or asphyxiate in falsehood.

For whatever madness now dictates to annihilate,
your assassination declares that the world changes inexorably,
                                    even without words.

WEEKEND IN LANGEBAAN

After a spell of staleness, something's quite exhilarating
about opening a door, entering into an odourless room
with beds covered in fresh linen edged with blue shells,
bouncy, clean pillows providing consummate comfort.

In the morning, Ron, the lanky owner, meditates on his deck.
We enthuse about the accommodation's fresh ambience;
he elaborates – with a wry smile – that he turned away from
'all the bullshit' sounding like an unrepentant rock star.

We stroll on the winding beach watching mists cascade,
early morning dippers frolicking in the surf,
children chasing tides under adults' watchful eyes,
wobbly, pink starfish iridescent in west coast light.

On the second day squawking gulls wake us,
we nibble cheese squares on toast, sip soothing Rooibos tea.
Ron quips that the TV remote had *vanished mysteriously*
and he had *thought* about replacing it!

That evening we submit to watching muted dramas on German TV,
and are for most of the night uncomplaining –
in between listening to crashing waves and resolving
to swim, sunbathe, unwind on the secluded beach after sunrise.

When we leave, Ron has vanished before we return his key,
so we take it to his neighbour completely in sync with the drill.
In his entrance hangs a saffron kimono and bright orange shawl
that welcome the uninitiated into Buddha's grace.

A PEDAGOGY FOR DEFIANCE

We had arrived at Kalk Bay beach,
spread our blanket on the pristine sand.
Our two boys, uncontrollably excited,
flung their beach tongs and dashed towards the sea,
when a red-faced harbinger appeared on the balcony
of the Brass Bell restaurant.

*Heh, julle behoort nie hier nie!**
Says, who? I defied challenging the callous prohibition.

He snarled, threatened to summon the police,
so we gathered our things and left
to save our sons further humiliation.

I had hoped that this degrading episode would be forgotten.
But forty years later, sitting round the table chatting,
my youngest son, unexpectedly, informed his wife:

*I remember us being kicked off the beach,
and my father confronting the owner of the restaurant,
not intimidated by him.*

At that moment, I recalled one morning when we arrived at school,
and discovered Mr Victor Wessels, my Afrikaans teacher,
had just vanished – denounced as a *persona non grata*
by apartheid security police. He was forced to work
in the rural town of Upington, or exit teaching!

Six months later, Vic reappeared in our class,
composed and ready to teach.
He greeted us, as usual, then asked:
'Now where did we stop the last time, class?'

Afrikaans: Heh, you don't belong here!

THE IMAM WHO DIED*

You were this nattily dressed man,
driving a shiny station wagon –
a 'salesman', someone informed us.

You lived in a stately, double-storeyed house
in Repulse Road, Sunnyside.
It stood out amongst the other ordinary homes
because of its balcony.

You were said to be prominent,
and I, as a teenager, measured stature
by the clothes you wore, the car you drove,
the neat, black, tassled fez that hajis don
perched on your head.

I could see you chose your outfits meticulously –
good colour co-ordination.

You always waved and smiled,
looking through the window driving past
as if you knew everyone.
I never saw your wife, your children,
you were always alone.

Then one day, my mother said:
*The imam who lives in Repulse Road
was killed by the boere;***
I didn't know about security police.
She added, *His kifaait will be today.****

Then I heard there was going to be a huge gathering
on the rugby field called City Park,
in front of our house in Rust Street.
But my mother ruled:
Don't go there kanallah****
it will be dangerous.
She didn't elaborate.

So I climbed onto our neighbour Mrs Finnan's back wall,
and looked over onto the rugby field.

There was a sea of white fezzes;
a bier covered with a black cloth and gold calligraphy
stood in the middle of the crowd like a precious gem
glistening in yellow sunlight.

The crowd was silent, until I heard voices
proclaiming about sacrifice
and greatness that never dies.

*Imam Haron who was murdered by the security police while in detention,
  27 September 1969
**Afrikaner police
***funeral
****please

WARRIOR*

Who said atheists do not believe?

You believed in duty,
    fulfilling your commitment
    though you did not seek solace in sanctified worship;

    cries of the poor were your litanies.

You believed in confronting deceit,
    strengthened us to disobey treachery
    despite the threat by miscreants waging unrest;

    fear, you taught, feeds stagnation.

Now we vacillate as falsehood flourishes,
    comrades with whom you resisted,
    now loquacious leaders parading as paragons for the oppressed;

    squabblers, out to enrich themselves.

---

*Dr Neville Alexander, activist, ex Robben Island prisoner, veteran socialist. Died 27 August 2012

HOW MEMORIES ARE MADE

You are now close to that timeless zone.
They say it's *stones in the gallbladder:*
an ultimate conspiracy against living things.

This morning, I observed the white lily
flourishing on my windowsill
had wilted into a funereal purplish-brown;
soon it will not glow in sprays of morning light,
but fall into fragile fragments before vanishing.

As the years fade, you'll not be asking me
what I am cooking or laugh at my menus:
memories coming and leaving arbitrarily.

PAX AMERICANA

You opened your gates to the desperate poor,
let them flock to your ill-begotten lands with illusions of liberty:
welcome to the home of the free and yankee-doodle-doo!

America,
you have become an old house overcrowded
with tyrannical turncoats and maladroit creeds,
stashed coffers with dead dollars by illicit bartering.
Where is peace and prosperity?

America,
Trump, your landlord, poses with a Bible in front of a church,
aping Verwoerd and his complicit apostles during apartheid.
Racism and hypocrisy reverberate in unholy kinships.

America,
spectres of Vietnam and atrocities stunt salvation.
A strong moral mudsill should be laid firmly
to secure a future for you and your squabbling children.

Welcome to the home of the free and yankee-doodle-doo!

QUESTIONS AND ANSWERS BEHIND WALLS

The wall is nine metres high.
I don't see a sun or a moon.

My father perished behind this wall
soon after he spoke those words.
They say he was a D-Voter.*

I am a D-voter, too, now.
There is a Detention Centre at Manas for us.
There is a Detention Centre in England, too,
the new depositaries for human strays,
boats overflow sinking with cries of the destitute
drowning in droves in a deluge in Pakistan.

Are you Muslim? They interrogate.
These questions are perpetual.
Has your identity been difficult for you?
What is your story?

What... IS... my... story...?
The world being curious yet hesitating to rescue its children,
that's my story.

Do you love India? The UK?
Their questions are not seeking any of my answers.

I live in Britain now, but I still feel Indian,
I tell myself quietly to calm my spirit.
Questions sustain what persecution cannot erase.

*D-Voter   Dubious Voter in Assam India, disenfranchised by the government on account of their alleged lack of proper citizenship credentials. They are sent to detention camps; some flee to the United Kingdom.

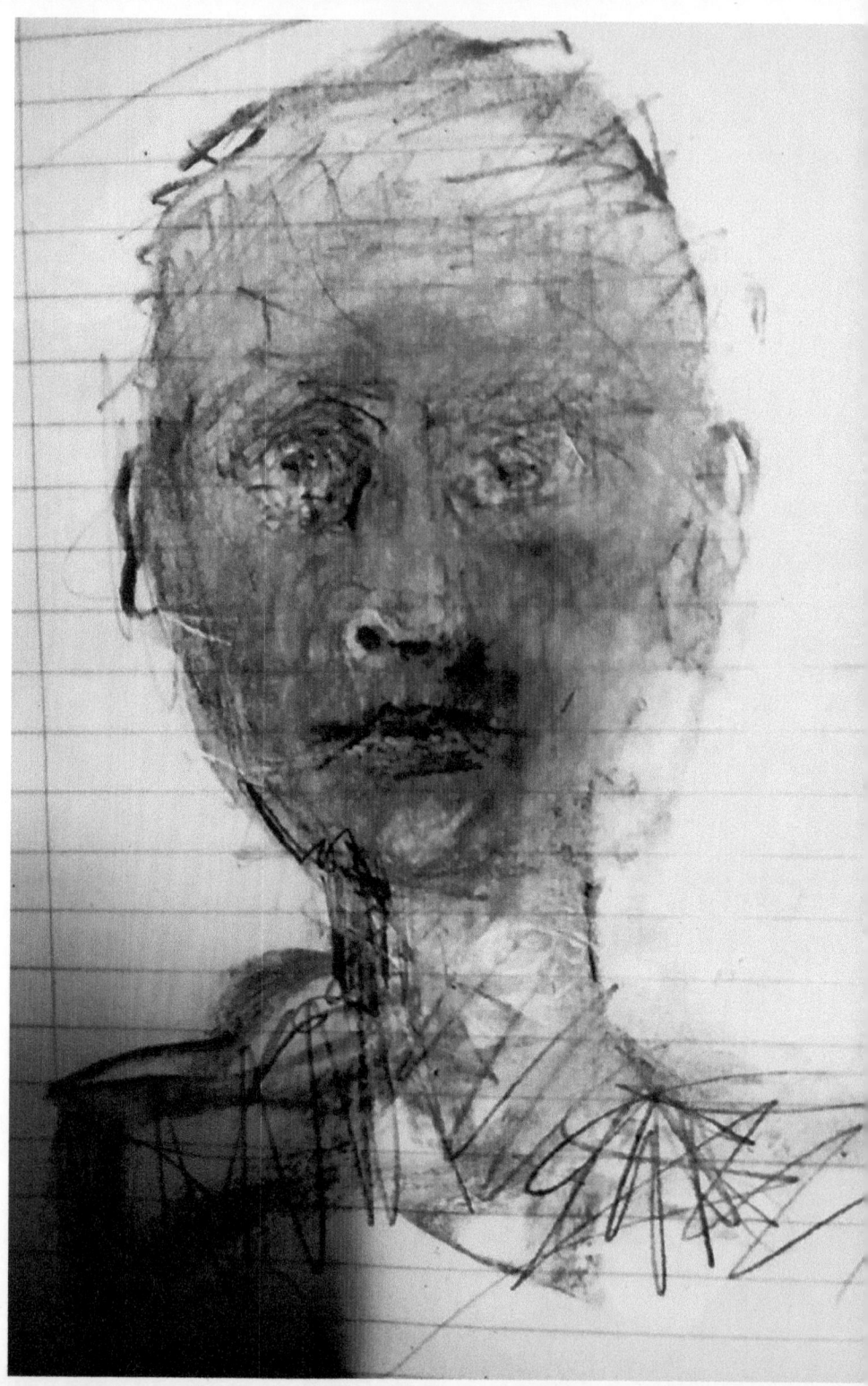

REMEMBERING ME
-for Rhoda Kadalie (1954—2022)

When you speak about me after my death
speak about me, not yourself
say how I am missed for things you didn't like
don't sanitise my memory by recalling only my virtues

let me stand between you and the line that divides us
just as I was, authentic, not some polite version of me

tell people how obnoxious I was at times, even offensive,
how I despised safe superficiality, political correctness

talk about all of me, not what you think you should say about me
that's right, don't speak politely to placate hypocrites

if you want to remember me

*Ms Kadalie was a well-known South African feminist, activist

NEW SOUTH AFRICAN PHOBIAS

Nowadays I am protected by burglar guards,
Trellidors, and an alarm system.
My considerate neighbour telephones me
when my system triggers and I am not at home.

A report about an aged couple bludgeoned to death
by their gardener frightens and disgusts.
He had toiled for them for years, was remunerated generously,
gifted clothes for his family.

I am contemplating using funds saved to visit Andalusia
to install electrical fencing around the house.

Maybe then I can keep hungry hearts and hands at bay.

REFORMS, REGRESS

Starless skies are ablaze with orange flames on university campuses,
books and artefacts furl in fiery infernos of frustration;
paradigms implode as misrule and stale reforms proliferate
into internecine violence and debilitating self-loathing.

The new leadership rearranges its deckchairs on a sinking ship,
their hapless hopefuls tweet in centres of lacklustre imbizos;
in this crippling conundrum many citizens call for the reinstatement
of the death penalty, corporal punishment to be meted out in schools.

NON-DELIVERY STAGNATION

I ruminate in a winding queue waiting
to buy bread and other groceries,
my hands clutching a newspaper.

More avaricious officials have dipped into state coffers
as the current leader announces job losses are looming:
ten million workers will face retrenchment.

Goods I bought provide tangible security for living
where I now hesitate to call safe
with simple necessities so few enjoy.

Delivery is sabotaged by bailing out pervasive incompetence.
Nepotism deters delivery as bereft municipalities
spiral into dysfunctionality.

PASSING TIME

I received a text from a friend declaring
she had decided to revamp her bathroom,
a project deferred for quite a while.

Nessie telephoned me later:
she had gone to pray for the entire world,
lit a candle for those who died during the pandemic.

I decided to address Azza about the pitfalls of pandering
to wayward children, then drove to Claremont
just to buy a box of ginger tea.

Peter says he needs to switch off from Trump –
an American imbroglio who could be around forever –
but is still driven to watch the news.

Passing time becomes an implacable pull,
even impelling a visit to a shop's shelves
to purchase winter boots in spring.

TRAIN RIDES WITH SASJA

Sunday afternoons, I loved taking you on rides to Simonstown.

I would piggyback you across the dry field next to Kromboom Road,
trudge to Crawford railway station.

It was our time away from home, our time alone,
to share our love for chook-chook trains!

I watched the joy in your face passing through platforms.

>   L-A-N-S-D-O-W-N-E
>   O-T-T-E-R-Y
>   S-T-E-U-R-H-O-F

You stared in amazement through the window
as tracts of land became shore and sea:

>   M-U-I-Z-E-N-B-E-R-G

Thrilled by the crash of high tide, waves pummelled walls along the tracks.

>   -T- J-A-M-E-S

Where is the missing S in -T? you would ask.

>   K-A-L-K B-A-Y

I would brush away the lush, brown curls from your doe eyes,
excitement widening them like a far horizon.

S-I-M-O-N-S-T-O-W-N!

Arriving at last, we would stroll on Long Beach,
and I never failed to coax:

Can you imagine how vast the ocean is?

At first, you didn't respond; then one afternoon you surprised:

It starts where we are standing and ends where the sea touches the sky.

I was moved by your succinct answer knowing you would soon seek answers to more vexing questions.

WALL OF DENIALS

It's easy to terrorise maps,
build a wall of denials to depopulate,
wipe a country into a blank space,
admit that Palestinians exist but not Palestine,
claim that God and imperial Balfour
gave you *fellahin** land
to compensate for Nazi evils.

This wall perpetuates atrocity
inflicted on thousands of the already dispossessed,
legitimates expedient Western pacts
with their clients, Arab oil barons.

This barrier –
        between interminable slaughter
          and the realisation of justice –
possesses another name.

*fellahin: (Arabic) peasants; used as a derogatory reference used by Zionists to describe indigenous Palestinians to justify their occupation of Palestine

AFTER THE FALL

You have toppled old edifices erected by colonialists,
smeared excrement over the vestiges of their violent past.

You have declared their demise in the battle for
bodies, hearts and minds
closed the chapters on their debauchery.

So who are we grooming to put in place?
What nascent visions will lead the trashed utopias?

What
will
fire
and
fury
feed?

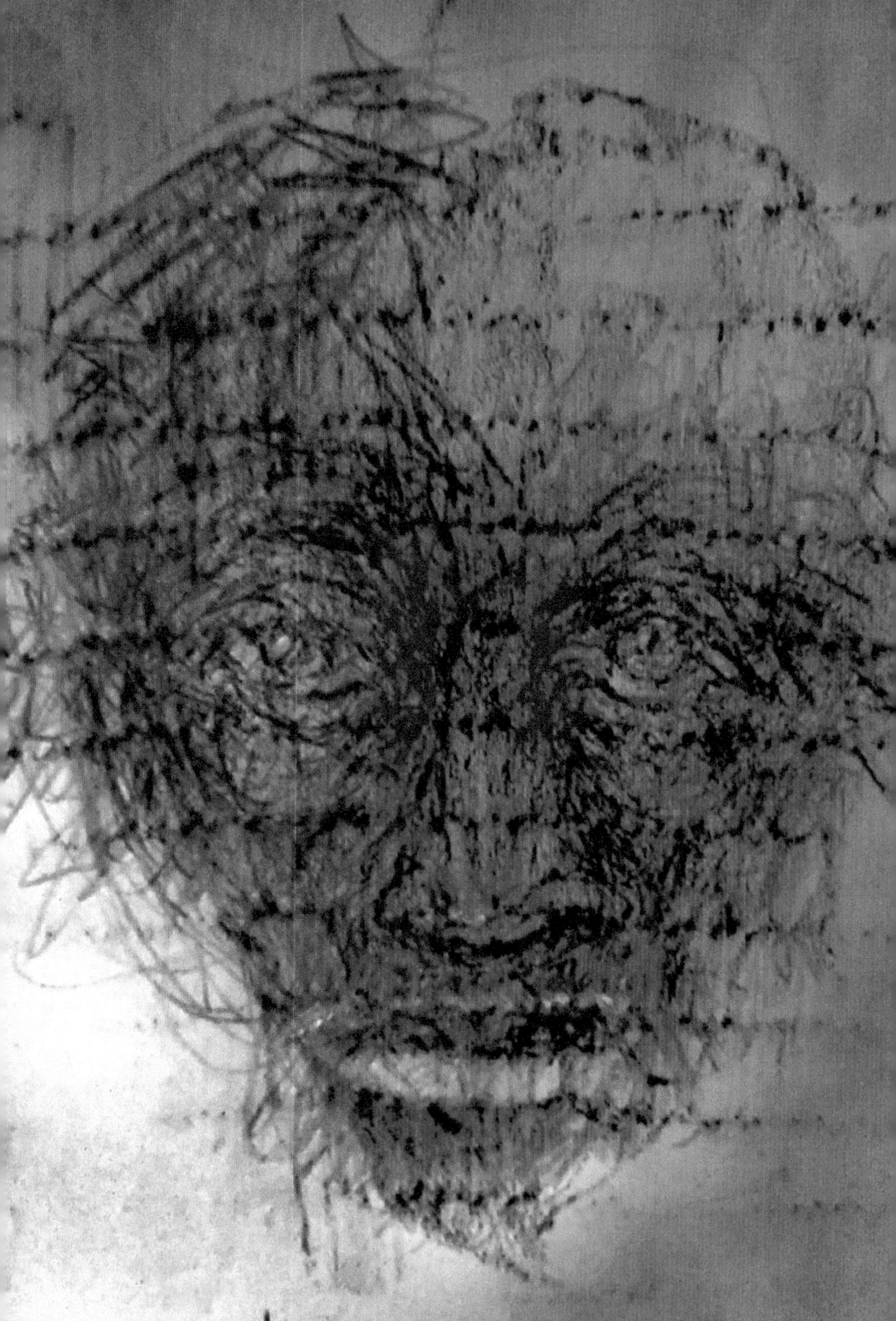

LUMUMBA'S TOOTH*

Sixty years later, the family of Belgian
police officer, Gerard Soete, accedes
to return Lumumba's tooth to relatives.
Colonialism exposes its crimes in such
aloof, unrepentant ways, staring stoically
at victims' indelible scars, unabated pain.

Soete's report:
*That's all that was left after his body
was burnt to ashes by unknown assassins.
Findings were inconclusive – to subject
a tooth to DNA analysis would destroy it,*
Juliana, his daughter, was informed.

Lumumba's resistance to imperialism
threatened the duplicitous schemes of
Western powers and their Congolese
sidekicks. Faceless pacts torched him.
A resilient tooth, preserved by an irony
surfaces, mocking barbarism.

Perhaps the new king Charles III will
return the brilliant Cullinan diamond
to South Africa, exquisite Ko-hi-Noor
stone to India. DNA tests will not be
required – we know where these belong.

*Patrice Lumumba was the first Prime Minister of the Independent Republic
of the Congo after its independence from Belgian colonial rule in 1960.

WHAT KIND OF LIFE IS THIS?

We march fiercely, ranting against Zionist zealots in Gaza,
clamour fiery slogans against persecution and dehumanisation in militarised Myanmar,
curse the United States as Mexican families are forced apart at the borders of affluent Califor

Yet we drive away from scuffles between shack dwellers and brutal police in trendy Sea Poir
look the other way when hunger stares, implores us at stop signs in the suburbs.

What kind of life is this, the one that we fill with many delusions so artfully?

SCHOOLBOY

Suffering's a decrepit figure on the pavement.
                I recognise that face.

Once you were a boy packing groceries at a Pick 'n Pay store
during school holidays, striving to combat privation.

Aged beyond years now, standing in front of a shop,
wholly neglected and grubby.

Once there was a hint of relief, but mercy shunned you:
the hopeful schoolboy transmuted
                into another wretched, waiting waif.

BURYING IAC*

Now that his body has left, we awaken gradually,
remembering from all quarters his concerns and causes,
scrambling for fervent teachings to inspire us to act decisively.

What went through the dying imam's mind just before he passed?
Did he look at those who surrounded him and think:
I know you'll be sad, but what will you lament?

Could he have foreseen that many who scorned his ideals,
would be paying homage at his funeral?
That they would say they admired his convictions, if only …
And how would he have felt listening to the bickering
about who his most loyal followers were?

I remembered this: heard it at a gathering when you spoke
soon after your release from Robben Island prison
relating that during incarceration a sparrow appeared regularly
chirping at your window.

You wondered what the tiny creature was delivering to you,
choosing to interpret these visitations esoterically.

*The late Imam Achmad Cassiem

JERUSALEM

*Where else are the vices to be found, but here in the holy city
where evil is in danger...*
										St Francis of Assisi

I

Jerusalem, where we hear ferocious war-hounds barking,
snarling with bloodthirsty, irredeemable venom
where slaughtering of children, evictions from homes, escalate.

II

Where under cerulean skies good and evil duel so vehemently
for the hearts and loyalties of the resilient who resist;
where blatant barbarism blasphemes under Zionism.

III

What better tainted terrain steeped in narratives of villainy?
What better streets stained with the blood of Golgotha?
What better city to burden us with the mayhem we unleashed?

NO LONGER A QUIET PLACE

We are leaving a quiet place,
those post-euphoria eras of ideals and allegiances
when we pledged blind loyalty.

Rampant ambition's unleashed
as orators for the working class sunbathe brazenly
with enemies in freewheeling Ibiza.

Betrayals defined as expedience,
strategic noises as corrupt officials infiltrate cities
while suffering and discontent reverberate.

HUNGRY PEOPLE DREAM

Citizens invade streets protesting
rising tariffs and food prices;

hungry people dream about bread.

Thousands of employed public servants strike
for wage increases;

hungry people dream about jobs.

Tenants clamour about increases in rentals,
rising interest on mortgages;

hungry people dream about shelter.

The Deputy President revels in a R37 million house
in an exclusive suburb, Waterfall;

politicians dream about dodging assassins.

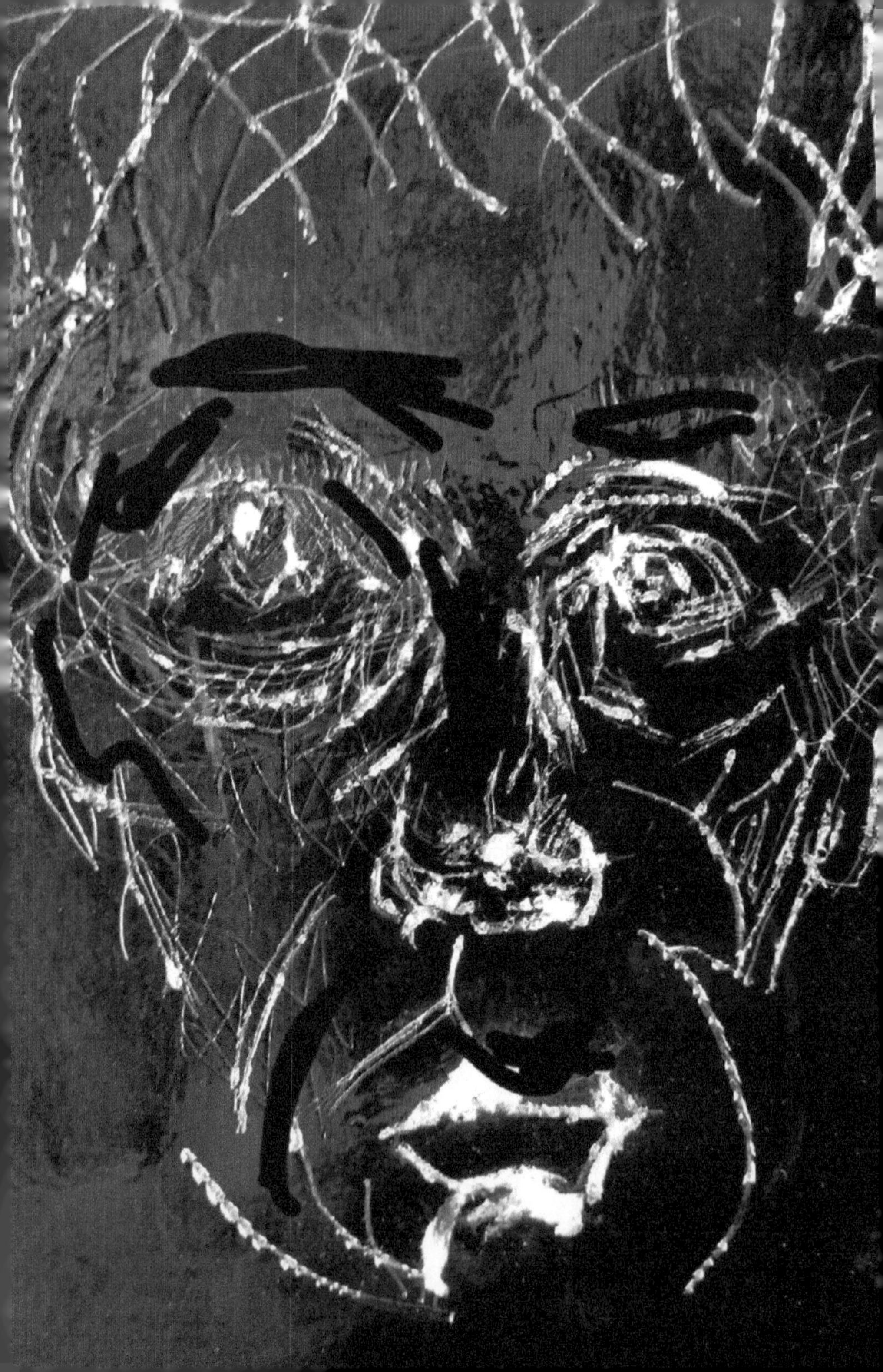

SINECURES AND HUSTLERS

Ploys are strategic modes for this new masquerade
as chicanery pretends there is order in chaos.

Power can feign a stance making it seem
you are fixing a fault with costly facades,
overdressing the hustler in deceptive overalls.

Dysfunctionality parades as gaining experience,
insidious, cold vanity and rectitude control
until the guile cracks and current marionettes pick puppets:

more brand-new sinecures from a posse of public servants.

TOMORROW'S JAILER

Pontificating today in your murky enclave of power,
you denounce all dissenters:

You are with us or against us.
There is no room for disagreement!

You have forgotten how you were degraded,
thrown like a rabid dog into a stinking cell to die.

Did safeguarding the wealth you hoarded so adeptly
mould you into this turgid turncoat?

Be mindful of the words you use
to safeguard present pervasive pragmatism.

Your orders echo old demagogues' degradation,
define you as tomorrow's jailer.

A DAY BECOMES IN SO MANY WAYS

Through a frosted window a moon slowly sails away

a sparrow sings its solitary tune so succinctly
                             and rouses

    silence is spirited away by dawn's stirring

the allure of fragrance permeating from your bathroom
                  awakens gently

soft murmurings of a nascent day fill the room
unobtrusively

    the dominant dark of yesterday's pervasive night
                    is duly vanquished

B.......... LIGHT

Does the pope's walk of words for his followers'
scandal of evil —
assimilate, you savage Inuit —
heal wounds ...

>   ?

Can the German nation's Nazi guilt ever pluck
their demons
from the gas chambers
of history ...

>   ?

Will Yale-groomed American presidents bring
reparation for the bloody sweat
of African slaves stripped and sold in the
colonies ...

>   ?

Who will clean the killing fields of Cambodia,
purge the blood-stained earth,
and placate haunting sorrows of the Khmer
and their Buddha's tears ...

>   ?

Will Truth and Reconciliation Commissions bring
deliverance to lives
forced into barren Bantustans and beer-stained rape,
tortured in detentions of the mind
and matter ...

                    ?

Who is the real enemy the mountain men
of Afghanistan are battling
when they veil and chain their girls and
women ...

                    ?

Can we expect to leave the shadows of chaos
or imagine we will ever be reprieved?
Why not sanction sin, commit abuse, as we ponder:
are we born free ...

                    ?

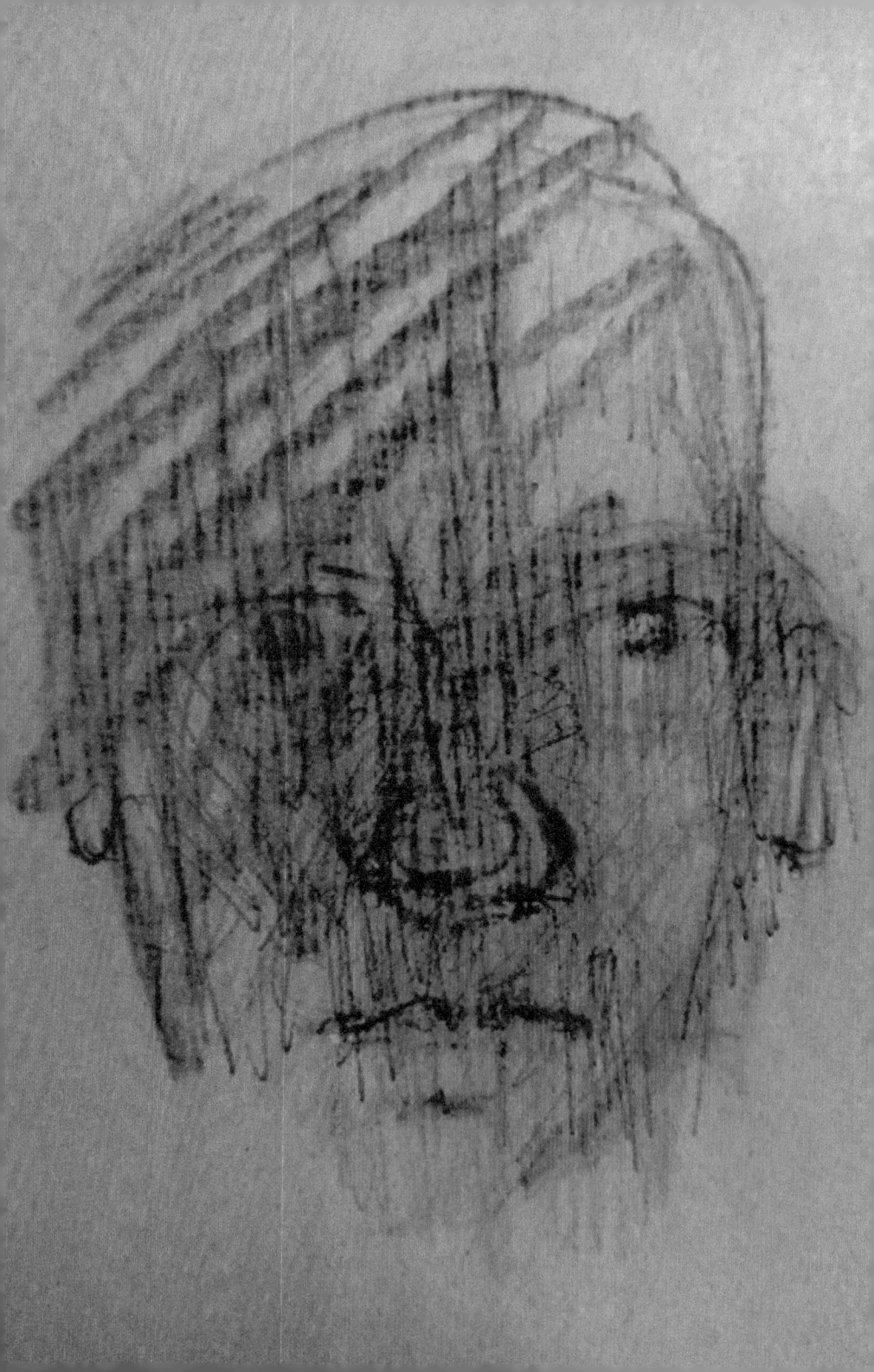

PAUSED TO SEE THE BEAUTY

I thought all was lost,
until I paused to see the beauty of the future
sparkling in my grandson's eyes, expressing:

There is still so much for me to do.

  Indecision lingered there,
before piercing the prose of certainty with unpredictability,
commensurate with a life yet unfolding.

  His eyes are not old men's,
desultory and remorseful, desperate for restitution,
recovering from chaos and calamities.

  I stopped to see the beauty in the stories we share,
nibbling at leftovers, recounting days
spent in battle – defeat and triumph.

  I thought all was lost,
until I paused to see the beauty in steadfastness and love,
to shift away memories of mishaps

and courageously forge ways to reimagine possibilities.

THE RUBBLE OF OUR LIVES

We have gathered the rubble of our lives;

what matters still is what lies in the terrain of ideals
where we will gather the broken shards
of love and old habits;

there is more to see, sift and cogitate later
with our eager hearts, fertile minds
and weighed words.

We assemble during a recess in a waiting room
of those mischievous muses,
seeing what we choose to see;

and concurring that nothing flourishes
outside the sum of the parts.

Abu Bakr Solomons worked as a teacher and principal for more than forty years in high schools and primary schools on the Cape Flats. He studied English literature at different South African universities and abroad.

A number of his poems were published in Tribute, Akal (journal of the Congress of South African Writers), The Poetry Institute of Africa, Botsotso poetry journals, Sol Plaatje European Union Poetry Anthologies, Sections of Six (Botsotso), New Coin (poetry journal of Rhodes University, Grahamstown) and New Contrast. A debut collection of his poetry and photographs, *A season of tenderness and dread* was published in 2016 by Botsotso. *Inhabiting Love* a second collection was published by Botsotso in 2020. *Rubble* is his third collection.